"When you change the way you see things, the things you see change."

–Anonymous

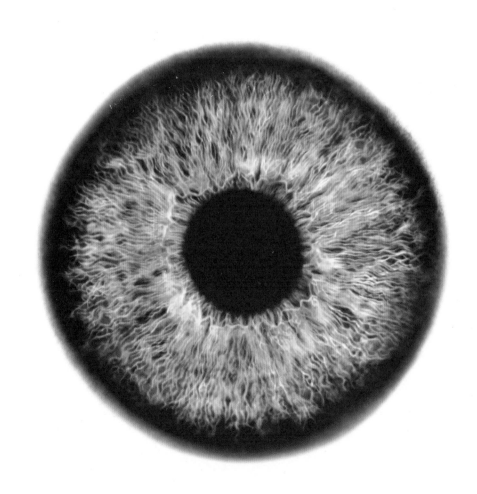

CHANGE
THE WAY YOU
SEE
EVERYTHING

THROUGH ASSET-BASED THINKING

KATHRYN D. CRAMER, PH.D.   **AND**   **HANK WASIAK**

Founder & Managing Partner The Cramer Institute LLC   *Co-Founder The Concept Farm*

Running Press
PHILADELPHIA • LONDON

Asset-based
Thinking

Asset-Based Thinking is the copyrighted property of:

© 2006 by The Cramer Institute and The Concept Farm
All rights reserved under the Pan-American and International Copyright Conventions
Printed in China

9   8   7   6   5   4   3   2   1
Digit on the right indicates the number of this printing

Library of Congress Control Number: 2005926446

ISBN-13: 978-0-7624-2723-9
ISBN-10: 0-7624-2723-X

Special Thanks to Getty Images. This book
could not have been done without them.

gettyimages®

Photos: Getty Images, unless otherwise noted
Photogenic by Jessica Crimmins
Photo page 6 by Sue Solie Patterson
Photo page 21 by Gosia Anna Kollek
Photos of Sonia Manzano, Linda Gray, Ed Marra and
Moby: personal photos unless otherwise noted
Photos pages 37 (Blocks), 39, 51, 60, 69, 77, 78-79,
114-115, 131 and 143 by Robert Singh
Photo page 60 (Sonia with Elmo) by Richard Termine
Photo page 83 by Dr. Margaret Guest
Photo page 140 by Suzy Gorman
Photo page 141 by Greg Lord
Photo page 142 by Russell Cole
Picture research by The Concept Farm
Cover design by Whitney Cookman
Interior design by The Concept Farm
Written by Kathryn D. Cramer, Ph.D. and Hank Wasiak
Edited by Jennifer Kasius
Typography: The Concept Farm
This book may be ordered by mail from the publisher.
Please include $2.50 for postage and handling.
But try your bookstore first!

Running Press Book Publishers
125 South Twenty-second Street
Philadelphia, Pennsylvania 19103-4399

Visit us on the web:
www.runningpress.com
www.assetbasedthinking.com

Foreword by James Patterson

Foreword by

James Patterson

I am often asked how I manage to write so many books. By way of explaining why I'm driven to it, let me tell you a driving story from my youth.

When I was growing up in Newburgh, New York, up along the Hudson River, my grandfather had a business delivering ice cream and frozen food. Most of his territory was a cluster of small villages on the other side of Storm King Mountain and occasionally he would bring me along.

Whenever we would go over the mountain, he would sing. He wasn't the best singer in the world, but he did it with great passion (and loudly) and one day I asked him why he was always singing.

And he turned to me and gave me the most important career advice of my life. He told me he didn't care whether I became President of the United States or a ditch digger or a truck driver like him. Only one thing was important: "When you go up over the mountain to work every morning, make sure you're singing. The same way I am in the broken-down ice cream truck. I am happy, Jim."

And that's the way I am about writing. Every morning when I go into my study and sit down to write I have a song in me.

When I read **CHANGE THE WAY YOU SEE EVERYTHING**, I saw that it does what it promises to do, and more. This is a simple, but brilliant thesis. Much like my grandfather's advice, it gives us information we can actually use.

James Patterson

HOW SMALL SHIFTS MAKE SEISMIC DIFFERENCES

IMAGINE THIS...

People from all walks of life (professionals in business, athletics, medicine and consulting, managers, mothers, fathers, teachers, journalists, administrators) surpass their current levels of excellence and achievement just by shifting, ever so slightly, the way they see everything.

Just think what could be possible if people focused their attention on:

- Opportunities rather than problems
- Strengths more than weaknesses
- What can be done instead of what can't

When you decrease your focus on what is wrong (deficit-based thinking) and increase your focus on what is right (Asset-Based Thinking), you build enthusiasm and energy, strengthen relationships, and move people and productivity to the next level.

DBT is hard wired...

Most of us are not accomplished Asset-Based Thinkers. Instead, we rely more heavily on deficit-based thinking (DBT). DBT concentrates on personal gaps and weaknesses, what is bothersome and irritating about others, and what is not working, problematic, and holding us back. Our reliance on DBT comes naturally. The human nervous system is hard-wired to be more sensitive to negative signals of impending danger than to positive signals of burgeoning opportunity.

In today's post-9/11 world of economic uncertainty, threats of terrorism, and alarming media headlines, we are constantly reminded of the potential negative side of virtually everything around us. No wonder people are more leery, skeptical, and worried than ever. As anxiety levels rise, deficit-based thinking becomes our "steady diet." But this steady diet of DBT leads to mental, emotional, and spiritual starvation. It zaps our energy and robs us of the enthusiasm and conviction we need to make the most of our own lives and positively impact the lives of others.

In spite of our biological programming, deficit-based thinking does not have to rule our minds, spirits, or actions. With concentrated, well-guided effort, we can regain energy, harness our inherent (albeit sometimes latent) optimism, and powerfully engage what life has to offer. All it takes is a shift (ever so slightly) in the way we see everything. **ABT is hard wired too.**

That is what this book is all about.

What is [ABT]

Asset-Based Thinking equips you with a special way of viewing everyday life that yields maximum returns on your investment of attention and effort. It changes the way you respond in the privacy of your own thoughts, in every conversation, interaction, and circumstance—to ignite possibilities. Asset-Based Thinking is a concrete, cognitive process aimed at identifying the assets (e.g., strengths, talents, synergies, and possibilities) that are immediately available in yourself, other people, and any situation.

In the light of opportunity, Asset-Based Thinking blocks out distractions and creates a focal point of concentration and high mental energy that keeps you alert and inspired until you have maximized all there is to gain.

In the face of problems or uncertainty, Asset-Based Thinking shows you how the glass can be "half-empty" *and* "half-full" simultaneously. (That is what makes Asset-Based Thinking practical and useful.) But Asset-Based Thinking also magnifies how to turn what is half full and half empty to your best advantage. (That is how Asset-Based Thinking produces dividends that just keep paying off.) Asset-Based Thinking increases your self-confidence, makes you more proactive and more effective with others, and expands your power to influence how things will turn out.

What [ABT] is not

Asset-Based Thinking is not blind optimism or magical thinking. It does not offer the quick fix or overpromise results. It's not based on theory alone. It's based on direct, systematic observation into how a growing minority of highly effective, satisfied people think, feel and act. Asset-Based Thinking takes "positive thinking" to a whole new level of engagement. While positive thinking calls for a positive attitude about life and the future, Asset-Based Thinking calls for positive action and traction in the present moment. ABT puts the power of personal, interpersonal, and situational assets in your hands so that you can make progress and create the future you most desire.

ABT is NOT DBT

In contrast to ABT, with DBT, we scan for interference, what is disturbing and not working. DBT works more like a defense mechanism, showing us the problem from a negative angle so we are able to solve or eliminate whatever impedes success. It puts us "on guard," fostering an anxiety that robs us of confidence, hope, and deprives us of pleasure and productivity.

Even though DBT protects us under dire circumstances, for most of us it has become an addiction that dominates our way of thinking. Unfortunately, a "steady diet" of DBT leads to starvation—a depletion in energy—creating suspicion that trouble, problems and disappointment lurk around every corner. We learn then to "keep our back up" as DBT fuels our insecurity. Left unchecked, DBT clouds our perceptions, blinds us to possibilities and limits our options.

DBT Message		ABT Message
Not this again...	• •	At least I know how to deal with this.
Watch out!	• •	Heads up!
Why didn't you...	• •	What was in your way?
That won't work!	• •	What could work?
Oh no! Not again...	• •	Things could be better, but I've seen this before.
I'll never make it...	• •	Put one foot in front of the other and move.
That's just the way it is...	• •	Whatever it is...I'll work with it.
That's impossible...	• •	What is possible?
It's not good enough...	• •	Forget perfection.
He's out of his mind!	• •	What makes him tick?
I'll never get this done!	• •	This will take longer than I expected.
This sucks!	• •	I'm disappointed.
What's the matter with me?	• •	What am I learning?
How could you let that happen?	• •	How could you have prevented this?
Once again, you've fallen short!	• •	Step back up to the plate.
Get out of my way!	• •	Here I come.
If only...	• •	Hindsight is 20-20.
They just don't get it.	• •	They disagree.
How did I miss that?	• •	I missed that.
Whose fault is that?	• •	What's done is done. Move on!
Why didn't I do this or that?	• •	What can I do better next time?
I can't.	• •	I will.
That'll never change.	• •	How can I get around this?

Sound familiar?
What are some others?

17

Great! Now let's focus on how to change...

Are you DBT or ABT? You decide...

When you make a splash, you could choose to...

[Deficit-Based Thinking]

[–] Hold your breath
[–] Pinch yourself
[–] Don't tell anybody
[–] Keep your head down and hope

[Asset-Based Thinking]

[+] Go with it
[+] Congratulate yourself
[+] Broadcast the good news
[+] Laugh, smile, and be grateful

When you make a mistake, you could choose to...

[Deficit-Based Thinking]

[–] Fault yourself
[–] Second guess your motives
[–] Tell yourself how clueless you were
[–] Learn: Always look back so it
   never happens again

[Asset-Based Thinking]

[+] Own it
[+] Make amends
[+] Say, "I should have had a V-8"
[+] Learn: Never look back, be bold,
   move on

ABT factoid

Freedom is Just Another Word for Nothing Left to Lose

If you are free enough to act independently of your environment, you will possess great stability in the face of deprivation, failure and loss. The humanistic school of psychology, represented by such theorists as Rollo May, Carl Rogers, Erich Fromm, and Abraham Maslow, espouses the view that a sense of autonomy contributes to self-esteem and that both help one to remain strong and healthy in the face of hardship.

Remember: The choice is up to you.

ABT is ready whenever you are...

Asset-Based Thinkers

Asset-Based Thinking calls for small shifts in the way we absorb, perceive, filter, and interpret. It changes the way we see everything, leading to dramatic improvements in the way we live. Asset-Based Thinking **zeros in** on what's working rather than what's not and favors inspiration and aspiration over desperation … and it is infectious.

Every day, the opportunity to engage in Asset-Based Thinking stands before us in all kinds of situations, good and bad, large and small. It leads directly to the thrill of victory, while sidestepping the agony of defeat.

After 9/11, Mayor Rudy Giuliani focused his thinking (and the media's attention) on making acts of heroism more meaningful than acts of terrorism.

Oprah Winfrey devotes her time and talent to spotlighting people who live lives inspired by purpose and passion, dispelling the myth that the drama of dysfunction is the only thing that sells.

You sit in a meeting, drained by people who are complaining and blaming others for mistakes, and you move the conversation in a different direction by asking, "How can this be the best problem we've ever had?"

www.**assetbasedthinking**.com
Visit the ABT website to share some wonderful experiences, stories, advice, and words of wisdom.

ABT is a Choice
not a personality trait

Everyday Examples of [ABT]

You sit down to dinner, and the conversation begins with complaints about the day. Then you shift and ask everyone to share the best thing that happened to them that day, encouraging them to relive the high points. Everybody at the table is "engaged." Dinner becomes another high point.

You face a serious setback in your business: Sales are down 20 percent. You bring the team together. Rather than dwell on what possibly could have gone wrong, you choose to build on past achievements and current capabilities that will move the team forward. By shifting from "react" to "rebound," the momentum builds.

A project is dumped in your lap with zero budget and due yesterday. You could beat your head against a wall, but instead, you decide to "just jump in and do it." With this new "will do" attitude, the project is finished in half the time. With your energy intact, you start something new and far more interesting and engaging.

Like a zoom lens, when you focus the majority of your attention on the Asset-Based zone of your experience, life draws you in: You feel more motivated and energetic, more purposeful and passionate. You become proactive and creative versus reactive. You are able to concentrate on making important things happen instead of preventing and correcting the bad stuff.

This book teaches you to tap the power of Asset-Based Thinking so that you can:

Change the Way You See Everything. . .

(+) **Change the way you see yourself**

(+) **Change the way you see others**

(+) **Change the way you see situations**

for the better, from this moment on.

the ABT ripple effect:

tap your personal assets first, all others will follow

relational assets

- compassion
- empathy
- mutual trust and respect
- commitment to the welfare of others
- skills in:
  - collaboration
  - giving and receiving feedback
  - resolving conflict
  - listening
  - advocacy
  - enrollment

personal assets

- purpose
- passion
- confidence
- curiosity
- resilience
- courage
- analytical and intuitive skills
- emotional intelligence
- subject matter expertise
- open-mindedness
- integrity
- ethics

situational assets

- challenges that promote breakthrough solutions
- setbacks that promote new standards of performance
- mistakes that offer new insights and learning
- opportunities that provide for innovation, mastery, and advancement

ESSENTIAL STEPS TO READING THIS BOOK

1 Take 45 minutes and read the book from start to finish—laugh, ponder, wonder—let it move you.

2 Mentally note every idea you agree with—put it into practice and give yourself an "A."

3 Stay open. Whatever you don't agree with, tough, try it for seven days and see what happens. You may be surprised. (Don't worry. You can always go back to your DBT ideas.)

4 Take notes, especially when something surprises you, catches your attention, or confirms what you already know. Write in the margins. This is your book!

5 Do the workouts and reflections. (Really!)

6 Make one change in the way you see yourself, other people, or situations, and practice that ABT approach twice a day for twenty-one days. (That's how long it takes to form a habit.)

7 Track your success and tell at least one person—more if you're ambitious.

You're well on your way to becoming an Asset-Based Thinker and changing the way you see everything! Get ready for the rush of energy—a definite by-product of ABT!

Browse, zoom, freeze, enjoy.

USE THIS BOOK

Each section lays out a simple but important aspect of Asset-Based Thinking that can be absorbed separately or taken in the context of the entire book. To really harness the power of Asset-Based Thinking, be sure you **connect the dots, page by page.**

Like the kid's drawing game, by connecting each idea to the other, you get a reward—you become an Asset-Based Thinker and discover a whole new pattern for living . . . and you join a very powerful group of positive co-conspirators who make the world a better place in which to live.

CHANGE
THE WAY YOU
SEE
YOURSELF

CHANGE THE WAY YOU SEE YOURSELF

Part I: Preview

The stories of David and Denise that follow illustrate how becoming proficient in Asset-Based Thinking begins with changing the way you see yourself. What you see, think, say, and do relative to who you are drives how you see other people and any situation you encounter. It's the foundation.

The principle, Magnify What's Best, Focus on What's Next, requires that you be keenly aware of who you are and what you want to achieve—even while navigating demanding, chaotic situations and responding to the priorities of others.

One secret to staying on course is to keep even your smallest achievements in the forefront of your mind. Make what you've been able to accomplish more important than what you haven't.

When you magnify what's best and focus on what's next, your personal sense of confidence and competence increases . . . automatically. You approach life from the inside out . . . not the outside in. You engage demands—even setbacks and mistakes from the perspective of how they can serve you and your priorities. You ask yourself, "How can I advance my agenda given the current set of circumstances?" Your day starts with envisioning what you see as possible, what you want, regardless of the current reality. Your vision guides you, speaks to you, coaches you on what to do next—all day long.

You set up a desire-driven way of navigating through the ups, and downs and proactively pursue things that ignite your interests, passions, energy, and ingenuity. You still respond to the needs and interests of others and the requirements of pressing circumstances, but you transform every encounter into fuel for advancing your agenda.

David's Story

Late one January morning, I was waiting motionless behind the curtain in a brightly illuminated corporate television studio in Cupertino, California. I heard the voice of the announcer say, "Ladies and gentlemen, it is my pleasure to introduce you to our commentator for this program on how to manage the marketplace, David Washburn." I was about to host my first hour-long seminar before a live studio audience of four hundred, simulcast to nine thousand viewers in offices throughout the country.

This was my make-it or break-it moment, but little did I know how much of a career-defining turning point this step onto the stage would be. I took a deep breath and as I stepped out to the stage, an acute sense of risk washed over me and took control of my thoughts. My moment to shine was quickly turning into an intimidating threat. But I was enough of a pro to also hear another, albeit much more distant, voice urging me to rise to the challenge.

I could feel the "threat vs. challenge" war waging inside me. Two separate visions were playing out. In one I saw myself tripping over words, losing my train of thought, and walking off stage. Simultaneously in the background, I saw myself composed and connected to the audience. My message and delivery were riveting. In that split second, I decided to filter out the images of failure and filter in the images of success. This change of focus allowed me to feel the challenge, not the threat. As I visualized the positive mental movie, I drew on my assets of experience, knowledge, and passion and forgot about everything else. A rush of confidence swept over me.

I refused to dwell on any aspect of threat. If the microphone went dead, or the cue cards fell over, or technicians scurried around behind the cameras, I told myself it simply would not make a difference. I went on stage and knocked 'em dead! After the presentation, I realized that this entire process happened in less than a minute and all it took was to make that one small shift to the asset side of the ledger. Everything else flowed after that.

Denise's Story

I left my job at the State Department and moved to the Midwest when my children were both under three to make it easier for my husband to become a partner in a top-tier law firm. I was thrilled at the prospect of raising Justin and Carly in a less hectic and more balanced environment.

For the first year, I was totally consumed with sizing up neighborhoods and preschools, renovating our new home, joining a church and swim club, and parenting Justin and Carly. I hardly had time to notice that while I was successfully creating the "almost perfect" domestic front, I was losing touch with myself and the professional career that had been my soul's work.

One afternoon when I was particularly down and exhausted, I decided to listen to my inner voice to gain some insight into how I might be getting in my own way. "You're having one more lackluster day," I recalled commenting as I picked up the thirty-first toy and put it into the basket especially for toddler fare. In there, we had one of everything proven to raise the IQ and EQ of our kids. "We have it all and we are organized!" I thought to myself.

As I listened to my internal bantering, I caught my tone of sarcasm—self-mocking, too close to self-deprecation for my own good. I wondered what had triggered this downward, self-deprecating spiral. Then I realized that I had been focused on everyone else's needs but my own, and I was feeling loss and resentment. I realized that the time had come to also put emphasis on what made me thrive and want to jump out of bed every morning. I could still be a first-rate spouse and mom but could also feel the passion for learning, leading, and contributing to the causes that have fed my soul for so many years.

I found out how to step into a book club, a neighborhood council role, and a volunteer position on the Regional Commerce and Growth Association. The cloud over my head began to lift, and I could feel my heart beating and my mind racing. I made my passions my priorities and they fueled a whole new way of looking at each day.

Magnify What's Best and Focus on What's Next

Picture the moment when a toddler takes her first steps. Imagine her parents' reactions—their fascination and excitement. Cheering is automatic. Criticism is nonexistent, wobbles and missteps are not even noticed. In your early years, it's impossible to learn, grow, or develop a positive sense of yourself without someone letting you know just how amazing and talented you are.
This is Asset-Based Thinking 101.

The next time you want the thrill of moving to the next level (so you can beat par, start a company, write a book, get a promotion, double your production, parent a teenager, lead an organization, or fall in love), remember this Asset-Based Formula that children follow instinctively:

(+) Set your sights on what you want/need.

(+) Move past fear.

(+) Start from exactly where you are with gusto and self-abandon.

(+) Practice as if no one is judging.

(+) Build on what you already know how to do—add, shape, edit, expand.

(+) When you experience victory, celebrate!

(+) Set your sights on the next step.

Please note: As an adult who wants to advance, you are required to play both the part of the toddler and the parents—who, by the way, cannot keep their eyes off of the talents, strengths, unique capacities, and strong desires of their undeniably gifted child.

ABT factoid

Desires Help Us Grow—In 1968, Abraham Maslow published his landmark text on how human beings develop and grow, *Toward a Psychology of Being*. Maslow became a major proponent of the theory that people grow in pursuit of such positive desires as safety, belonging, respect, prestige, and love. He contended that the realization of this hierarchy of desires results in self-actualization, a state of high satisfaction, autonomy, and mastery.

Forget Perfection

Asset-Based Thinking liberates you from the pointless need to strive for "perfection." You realize that pursuit of perfection is not an asset, it's a liability. For a change in the way you feel about yourself, see yourself as a work in progress . . . just like everyone else. Each day, say to yourself that for today you are perfect the way you are. Always competent, yet always learning, always growing. Commit to making the most of yourself and you will find that flaws will fade away.

WARNING: A preoccupation with eliminating flaws invites self-absorption, whereas recognition and reconciliation with shortcomings promotes a healthy and powerful humility that liberates you to move forward.

TRY THIS: Make a mistake on purpose. Commit an error that detracts from your effectiveness. Investigate where that leads you.

* Drive the "wrong way" to work so that it takes twice as long. Find out what you appreciate about the new route and extended travel time.

* Turn to the "wrong" section of the newspaper, something you normally wouldn't read. Scan the headlines and discover something cool you never would have found before.

Guarantee: Self-awareness will never lead to self-absorption. It will give you healthy amounts of self-respect and confidence so that you can achieve more, contribute more, and live a more inspired life.

41

$$\frac{(Judgment + Skepticism)}{(Reactivity)} = \text{ANXIETY}$$

Bypass Anxiety. . .
Build Energy

(−)

Deficit-based thinking is addictive. It keeps your adrenaline pumping and all of your sensory systems operating on Code Red. This mental, physical and emotional reaction tells your senses you are prepared and ready to meet the next crisis, setback, or problem. If you are like most people, you have grown to crave the adrenaline rush that comes from functioning on guard. But left unchecked, this can lead to constant anxiety, another by-product of deficit-based thinking. It is a totally negative addiction that depletes us and blinds us to the better side of reality—the side that keeps us in pursuit of possibility, opportunity, and reward.

(+)

Asset-Based Thinking is addictive too, but it is a **positive** addiction with affirming impacts. The adrenaline by-product of Asset-Based Thinking is pure energy—not anxiety. Asset-Based Thinking produces an intellectual rush that serves your positive aims. Asset-Based Thinking keeps your senses on high alert, not high alarm. All systems are go. Your mind scans for the best of what can happen next. Energy is flowing through your entire body. Your imagination is turned on. You visualize what is possible. You see how capable you are and how resourceful others can be.

When you cultivate an Asset-Based Thinking addiction, you satisfy cravings that bypass anxiety, build energy, and bring you to a wonderful state of being.

Make Assets Your Adrenaline

Interestingly, Asset-Based Thinking is more rational and realistic than idealistic and emotional. It provides a balance to the overly negative deficit-based images we typically have of ourselves.

Asset-Based Thinking provides you with a view of yourself that allows you to clearly see your strengths, skills, talents, and virtues. This Asset-Based point of view does not deny your weaknesses, faults, or shortcomings. It merely shifts your attention away from the negative energy they produce. It puts them into an Asset-Based context so you become less critical and more curious about how to counteract and compensate for personal deficits.

The more you draw on the power of your personal assets, your self-respect and confidence will grow dramatically (guaranteed). Being more in touch with all of your assets distances you from your flaws and diffuses their power to hold you back. You will be better at excelling under pressure, realizing untapped potential, developing rewarding relationships, and living a richer more worthwhile life. There will be no stopping you.

Try This: Think about who you are and how you add value. Make a list of at least five personal assets (strengths, talents, skills, and virtues) that make a significant contribution to your effectiveness. Next, think of one deficit (limitation, shortcoming, or weakness) that is the most significant barrier to your effectiveness. Now think about the challenges and opportunities you currently face. How can you leverage the five personal assets you have listed in meeting your challenges and realizing your opportunities? This is called the five to one rule. Focus on five assets for every one deficit. Put this rule into practice to build your own momentum and the momentum of others who matter to you.

"Your true passion should feel like breathing; it's that natural."

– Oprah Winfrey

Leap Out of Bed with Your Vision Turned On

The difference between a person who is vitally engaged in life and someone who is merely going through the motions is a vision fueled by passion. Side effects of this kind of vision may include:

- enthusiastic mood
- confident posture
- that look of being "up to something"
- an optimistic, energetic presence
- unbridled conviction
- undeniable magnetism

Having vision fueled by passion promotes a special kind of *vision*—it's a "seeing" that makes the future seem tangible and well within your grasp. You can feel, hear, taste, and see all that you desire. It is the source of being vitally engaged!

Try This: Morning Mental Workout

Begin each day with a mental workout. Coach your first thoughts to be strong, clear, encouraging. This morning routine will keep you from wanting to roll over and go back to sleep. It is a vivid dress rehearsal that shapes what you aim for and how you respond to what comes your way.

Review your most important objectives by completing the following sentence: "I am the perfect person to accomplish_____ because I am/have_____."

Describe your objective   Describe your assets

Repeat three times. This dose of Asset-Based Thinking will remain active for up to 24 hours.

Knock Somebody's Socks Off

Try This: Tell yourself an Asset-Based bedtime story. Just before you fall asleep, review the day's events and create a story from the point of view of how you realized your vision. Recount the goals you pursued and how you made strides. Note all tangible evidence of success. Ask yourself, "Whose socks did I knock off today?"

Hold That Vision No Matter What

Challenges to your vision come in all forms, from any direction, and at all times. It's life—conflicting demands, unexpected down turns, changing of the guard, even innovations that change the competitive landscape and may lure you off your vision's course. But when your vision is fueled by your personal passion, it is unswerving, unstoppable, always in focus, immune to distraction, and never in doubt.

LET PASSION
BE YOUR POWER

Josef Szajna

A Polish painter, leading designer and director of avant-garde theatre, he survived Auschwitz and Buchenwald. While in the concentration camps, Szajna was confined to a "standing cell," which was four feet by four feet, made of cinder block, no windows, with a ceiling open to the sky. These cells housed four prisoners.

Descriptions of Szajna's dedication to his art are amazing. Suffering many sleepless nights, Szajna used those periods to advance his skill and to build his portfolio of paintings. He stood motionless in the cold, crowded cell and fired his imagination with the work that excited him most. His caring for representing the beauty of landscapes and skyscapes guided his vision.

Night after night, Szajna painted minds-eye paintings. He visualized his palette, brushes, oils, and canvas vividly, thoroughly. Every detail of his movement unfolded like a movie in his mind. He created and catalogued space for wet canvases to dry. Painting was Josef Szajna's passion. He never stopped pursuing his vision even while confined and deprived of the most basic tools he relied upon. Josef Szajna said that passion and belief in himself as an artist saved his sanity and his life.

> *Reflect:* **What visions do you have? What passions fuel them? We all have them in us.**

REFLECTION

1. Make a list of three to five things you have accomplished in the past week or so. (Note: Most of us did not receive a Nobel Prize yesterday, so don't be concerned with the magnitude of your accomplishments. List those that stand out.)

2. Now, reflect on the personal talents, strengths, and skills you used in making those accomplishments happen. Jot those down next to each accomplishment.

3. Take a good, **long** look at your notes. This is your ABT profile. What patterns do you see? Think about how you can leverage this particular positive pattern of skills, talents, and strengths—today, tomorrow, and next weekend! Do this reflection on a regular basis and you will be amazed at what you discover about yourself (We all have major blind spots when it comes to our own unique assets).

ACCOMPLISHMENTS	TALENTS, STRENGTHS, SKILLS
1	
2	
3	
4	
5	

notes:

ABT factoid | **You are what you feel** — A study in the August 2002 issue of "Mayo Clinic Proceedings" reported that people who expect misfortune and see the negative side of life (the DBT crowd) don't live as long as those with a more optimistic view. Additionally, these Asset-Based Thinkers had fewer problems at work and in other daily activities, less pain and fewer emotional problems, and increased energy.

ABT
WORKOUT
1

ABT principle: Magnify What's Best, Focus on What's Next

The principle Magnify What's Best and Focus on What's Next requires you to be keenly aware of who you are and what you want to achieve and contribute—even while navigating demanding, chaotic situations. Sometimes, it's tough to be even dimly self-aware, much less to be keenly self-aware.

When you get so busy juggling the deluge of pressures and demands that come from others, your own priorities suffer. You are more reactive than proactive. Being reactive promotes self-criticism and feelings of being "behind the eight ball." Being proactive increases a personal sense of confidence and competence.

When you magnify what's best and focus on what's next, you are proactive. You approach life from the inside out . . . not the outside in. You look at demands—even setbacks and mistakes—in terms of how they can serve you and your priorities. You scan your environment and ask yourself, "How is it possible for me to advance my agenda given the current set of circumstances?"

Your day starts with envisioning what you see as possible, what you want, regardless of the current reality. You let your vision guide you, speak to you, coach you, tell you what to do next—all day long.

You set up a desire-driven way of navigating through the everyday ups, downs, and plateaus, and you proactively pursue things that ignite your interests, passions, determination, commitment, energy, and ingenuity. You still respond to the needs and interests of others or to the requirements of pressing circumstances, and you transform every encounter into fuel for advancing your agenda.

Magnify What's Best and Focus on What's Next

Step I: Mentally assign yourself two different roles: **"The Observer"** and **"The Navigator."** The Observer's job is to monitor the ratio of proactive to reactive behavior. The Observer is your most valuable asset for developing self-awareness. The Navigator is the part of you that intentionally, purposefully moves through the day. The Navigator is you, the person who absorbs, filters, interprets, thinks, speaks, acts, and interacts.

Step II: Throughout the course of your daily activity, periodically check in with The Observer to register how proactive you have been. Ask The Observer, "How have I devoted my time and attention to my highest priorities? How have I kept my priorities in mind while responding to external demands?"

Note: The best way to foster proactive self-awareness is to catch yourself in the process of doing just that. Attitudes and behaviors that you recognize and confirm will deepen and become even stronger.

Step III: Whenever you get caught in a reactive spiral, pause. Ask your Observer, "What personal skills and capabilities do I have that can help me shift from reactive to proactive?" You might find out that your ability to concentrate, or to "say no," or to show compassion, or to ask for time out are at your disposal, ready to help you be more proactive than reactive.

Step IV: Reflect on your day. Give yourself points for being self-aware and proactive. Count the ways you authored your existence by influencing what happened next. Remind yourself of the moments when you let who you are and what you want to achieve and contribute guide you and show you what to do.

Note: People who have better recall for episodes of success than for episodes of failure are more optimistic, self-confident, and effective.

SONIA MANZANO
Actress, Writer, Designer, Role Model

Sonia Manzano has inspired and entertained kids for more than thirty years. Known to us as Maria on Sesame Street, Sonia has been a passionate advocate for the positive portrayal of Hispanics in communications. In this interview with Hank, Sonia reveals how her role on Sesame Street led to new and ever better ways of seeing herself . . . her heritage, her talents, her opportunities. Enjoy this glimpse into the mind and heart of an Asset-Based Thinker who keeps on reinventing herself.

Hank: On Sesame Street, you went from being in front of the camera to behind the camera. You started writing. How did you make that shift?

Sonia: I felt the segments that addressed Hispanic culture could've been better so I set out to write some of those segments myself. That made me realize what the producers were up against. They had to produce a show that was funny and educational that a child and an adult would enjoy. I felt empowered because I knew I could deliver what they wanted.

H: What sparked your feelings of empowerment? What about your childhood was a catalyst?

S: When I was a kid I was influenced by everything I saw on television. Not seeing anyone like me made me wonder how I could contribute to a society that didn't seem to see me. So when I write for Sesame Street, I always think of myself as a kid in the audience... in my case the little Puerto Rican girl growing up in the Bronx. Everything that I've written for Sesame Street has that "me" in mind.

H: Other than Maria, who is your favorite character to write for?

S: Oscar the Grouch. Easy. Hands down, because the Grouch is either eight or forty-eight years old. I can be more free with a character who works on several levels.

H: You wrote a fantastic children's book called *No Dogs Allowed*. It feels autobiographical.

S: It absolutely is. I'm retelling an event that happened in my old neighborhood. (A neighborhood that now feels small, but I remember as being huge.) It's funny—my mother remembers those times as being tough. I remember them as being wondrous as well. Hispanics have very strong family, ties, traditions, and rights of passage.

In writing this book, I drew on my own experiences so that kids can hopefully appreciate their own "traditions," whatever they might be.

H: Often, when people meet you they call you Maria and relate to you as her. So you have to be proud of me. I haven't called you Maria once.

S: Bravo!

H: Now I want you to be Maria!

S: Maria is exactly like me and certainly everything that I've written for Sesame Street has a little bit of my background in it. But, when I first started I thought of her as a character and wondered how she should be. Then I realized what the audience and producers wanted. They wanted a real deal Puerto Rican. I think a reason that the show is so successful is that we strive to show real people. Kids get to see real life. When I fell in love, got married, and had a baby in real life we created dual plotlines on Sesame Street.

You could say we were the first reality show.

H: Actress. Writer. Now, a designer and entrepreneur. You founded a design company called "The 3 Amigas."

S: You can't help notice the Latin sensibility that is permeating many aspects of our culture. Music! Fashion! Food! I started thinking about the colors of my childhood. The tenement building doors that opened into Caribbean colored apartments. The 3 Amigas design company was born. We have a line of dishes, children's clothing, hats, and accessories. We hope to grow into a brand for the whole "familia."

H: You will always be "Maria," but "Sonia" is an even more inspiring and positive role model, what's next for you?

S: Another children's book called *A Box Full of Kittens* and I'm working on a memoir.

H: Great. Thank you, Sonia.

And one more thing. Give my regards to Oscar.

S: You got it!

Let Sonia's story remind you that seeing and believing in your assets, what makes you "you," is the gift that "keeps on giving." In Sonia's case her deep respect and value for her Hispanic heritage, her talent as an actress, her empathy and compassion for children who feel marginalized, and her desire to be creative are the combination of assets that fostered new careers and new heights of achievement throughout her life. Now that you've read Part 1, be sure you identify your unique combination of assets that promote your success and create a rich, rewarding life.

www.**soniamanzano**.com
Check out Sonia's website.

CHANGE THE WAY YOU SEE OTHER PEOPLE

CHANGE THE WAY YOU SEE OTHER PEOPLE

Part II: Preview

When you read Julian Fifer's story, you will see how he created visions that are as irresistible and compelling to other people as they are to himself. Whenever possible, Asset-Based Thinkers set goals that inspire other people to new heights of motivation and achievement. This approach is the place to start. It is easier to see and tap the talents and skills of your constituents when they are ready and eager to jump in.

It is far more difficult to view people through a positive, Asset-Based lens when they are turning away from your ideas or are in conflict with your direction. John's story illustrates just how tough and challenging a task this can be.

Part II illuminates how to use positive filters to get more traction when interacting with other people of all types and persuasions. It shows you how to re-activate a special instinctive positive filter that we are all born with. Over the course of life, your inborn positive filter has been overshadowed and shut down by deficit-based thinking, so you have to reactivate it. Your ABT filters will energize your encounters with people with a spirit of praise and acknowledgement for what they have to offer.

You will see each individual as an asset and recognize that he or she is a work in progress, just like you are. ABT encourages you to compliment out loud, often and to notice others in acts of generosity, brilliance, and productivity. The value you discover in people will stay with you so that you can build on these relationships over time.

There is another bonus that comes from ABT. You will be relatively unaffected by the angry outbursts, accusatory language, difficult behavior, and scapegoating of others. Instead, you will be able to deflect their disturbing behavior, suspend judgment, and investigate the interests, needs, and motives beneath the surface that fuel this negative behavior.

John's Story

I'm one of those fortunate business-men who works with a "coach" to help guide me through rough waters. I vividly remember the most productive long-distance session I ever had with her like it was yesterday. On a rainy afternoon at JFK, I placed a call to my coach, Judy, just before boarding a 737 back to St. Louis. When she answered, I didn't even say hello and asked her, "How do you dance with Attila the Hun?" She recognized my voice immediately and sensed my frustration tinged with my unique brand of sarcasm. Judy picked up on this and replied, "Who would have guessed that you would be the one to discover Attila the Hun alive and well in Manhattan?"

66|

That was just what I needed. "Attila's first name is Mike and every day he commits verbal acts of carnage from his executive suite on Madison Avenue." We both laughed. Judy knew that I didn't rattle easily but she sensed that Mike (...Attila) had thrown me off my game. So, I talked fast and she listened.

I explained, "Mike is a classic adult bully who attacks anyone in his way. He wrestles the goods away from you, insults you to your face, and steps on your reputation with your clients. I can't work with this SOB. No trust, no tango."

Judy dispensed with the small talk. She felt my pain and knew I needed support. She told me a story. In 1964, Thich Nhat Hanh, an exiled Vietnamese Buddhist priest, traveled to Washington, D.C., to solicit congressional support for a cease-fire to help end the Vietnam War. Senator Barry Goldwater opened his inquiry by asking Thich Nhat Hanh, "Are you from the North or from the South?" He answered, "Neither. I'm from the Center." Judy repeated his response to Goldwater's question twice. "Neither. I'm from the Center. Neither. I'm from the Center."

I said, "Great story, but what does it have to do with me and Attila?" Then we were cut off. On the plane, into my second bag of peanuts, I realized the simple yet profound wisdom in Thich Nhat Hanh's response. With that one statement, "Neither. I'm from the center," he shifted the framework of everything that would follow from negative to neutral, or the center. I started to see Mike as inherently adversarial, always looking for the next enemy. I didn't have to be "for or against him." Yes, he hammered first, but there was no reason for me to "take the bait" and step into the fight. By stepping into the mindset of Thich Nhat Hanh ("the center") in my dealings with Mike, many more creative options opened up. Rather than putting my energies into how I could kick Mike's ass, I thought about how to minimize the damage he caused and use his destructive tactics to my benefit. He wasn't going away, so I had to change my view of the situation and take action.

Liberated from this "war" mentality, I laid out my own plan to take the focus off of Mike. First, contact my colleagues who needed to be advised about Mike's latest moves. Second, call a meeting to solicit ideas for regaining the ground we may have lost with clients. Next, keep people's attention focused on ways to use Mike's meddling to actually strengthen client relationships. I became energized, more optimistic, and even eager to turn Mike's "lemons into lemonade." Now I was playing by the rules of my game . . . not Mike's.

When I got back home and checked my voice mail, there was a message from Judy. She was concerned that she hadn't given me enough time on the phone. If only she knew how much she said to me with those few words... **"Neither, I'm from the center."**

Julian Fifer's Story

Classically trained musicians spend years honing their individual technical prowess and interpretive skills in conservatories. Often they find themselves ill equipped to play in a large orchestra where they must submit to the authority of a baton-waving conductor. In a study he conducted in the early 1990s, a Harvard psychologist, Richard Hackman, found that job satisfaction among musicians in 78 orchestras in four countries was so low that they matched the same negative job satisfaction levels as federal prison guards!

Julian Fifer's inspiration for founding the Orpheus Chamber Orchestra came from his days at Juilliard where he experienced an inspiring intimacy and camaraderie among his peers. He became committed to re-creating the Juilliard brand of teamwork on a larger, grander scale. Fifer set his sites on establishing an orchestral organization within which communication and cooperation could flourish—without a conductor!

He essentially turned all the musicians into an improvisational network of collaborators. Rehearsals became free-for-alls in which all 27 members of the orchestra participated in every decision about every detail of nuance, phrasing, and dynamics. It quickly became clear that trying to make all decisions unanimous was unworkable, so he divided the orchestra into core groups whose members would rotate regularly. Each group rehearsed its own formulation of a piece and presented it to the larger group.

Another innovation came in the area of sharing leadership. In conductor-led orchestras, the role of the concertmaster is similar to that of a team captain. In Orpheus, the role is like a player-coach and is rotated. The concertmaster is responsible for running rehearsals, moderating debates, and negotiating solutions. Not only do the core groups and concertmasters change from concert to concert, they also change from piece to piece. This inclusive process allows each player to experience intense leadership training.

With the vision of a collaborative, high-spirited culture in mind, Julian Fifer and the orchestra members have established a financially robust, award-winning chamber ensemble. Orpheus has won world acclaim for artistic excellence with an unusually high level of professional satisfaction for its members.

Use Your Positive Filters, Get More Traction

Asset-Based Thinkers learn how to reactivate the special instinctive positive filters that we are all born with. Over the course of our lives, the positive filters have been overshadowed and shut down by deficit-based thinking. Asset-Based Thinkers approach everyone they encounter with a spirit of acknowledgement and praise for what they have to offer. They see each individual as an asset and recognize that they are a work in progress, just like themselves. They're not afraid to compliment out loud and often. Not only do Asset-Based Thinkers notice others in acts of generosity, brilliance, and productivity, the value they discover in those people stays with them so that they can build on the relationship over time.

Asset-Based Thinkers are relatively unaffected by the negative traits of others. They've learned to deflect the negativity, suspend judgment, and go beneath the surface to make contact with the positive motives that are fueling the negativity.

GET A CHARGE
OUT OF CONFLICT

Make Opposition Matter

Conflict magnifies and illuminates who you are. It seizes and startles you into seeing what makes you uncomfortable. It pushes your boundaries—intellectual, emotional, and physical. Conflict, if treated properly, offers the chance to change your mind altogether.

When faced with conflict, explore the possibility that opposing forces can both be true simultaneously. Taking this perspective immediately dissolves animosity and piques curiosity. You find yourself wondering, "What's their truth? Where is the value on their side?" When you finally give up the belief that yours is the only truth, it changes the game forever. Now you're in a position to see **what new truth you can create together.**

focus + distance = clarity

Deconstruct to **Reconstruct**

(−) **Deconstruct:** You can diffuse your negative reactions by asking yourself, "What would I be thinking or feeling if I behaved that way?" Once you realize that disturbing or irritating behavior is an integral part of everyone's repertoire, you can be less reactive. You begin to accept people for who they are and aren't. You facilitate constructive relationships.

Reconstruct: Use Asset-Based Thinking to replace the picture you have of the other person's negative attitudes and behaviors. Remind yourself of his or her strengths and most attractive qualities. Bring a more accurate picture into focus based on the positive assessment. This new point of view is an asset to moving forward in the relationship. (+)

Tell the Truth, Fast

Use Asset-Based Thinking to give constructive feedback that will have an impact and be heard over the noise of the defense mechanism. Take all the time you need to formulate your messages. Then, tell the truth fast.

People shy away from telling the truth when it might cause hurt feelings, trigger anger, or disrupt a relationship. They hold back the feedback that could help another person change and actually strengthen a relationship because they don't want the conversation to backfire. Deficit-based thinking takes over.

Take an Asset-Based approach by realizing that having a difficult conversation is a way to break through problems and move on to opportunities ahead.

Tell the truth fast: When confronting difficult topics, Asset-Based Thinking fosters speedy resolutions and diffuses negative inter-actions. To begin a healthier dialogue, follow these three steps. (Be sure to formulate and rehearse the conversation to start and end positively):

1. State the behavior that bothers you clearly and concisely.
2. State the impact of that behavior on you and the relationship.
3. Present the positive vision you have of resolving the conflict or disruptive interactions.

(+) The positive note you end on will set the tone for the action of the listener. Then, relax and enjoy what happens next.

RAISE THE COLLECTIVE IQ

"In everyone's life, at some time, our inner fire goes out.
It is then burst into flame by an encounter with another human being.
We should all be thankful for those people who rekindle the human spirit."

–Albert Schweitzer

Everyone Starts With an "A"

When Benjamin Zander, conductor of the Boston Philharmonic Orchestra, teaches new students, he begins the semester by giving everyone an "A." His tangible regard for the skill and potential of each individual propels their learning and expands self-confidence. They are motivated to do what it takes to retain the "A." It also builds an immediate bond and collaborative climate both with the teacher and among high-achieving artists who would normally be autonomous and competitive.

Try this: The next time you are with a group of people (business meeting, family dinner, little league game, cocktail party, etc.), look at each person and take note of what you like or admire about that individual. Be specific. Select any type of characteristic, from appearance to intelligence to virtue, to skillfulness. Do this immediately before you speak to the person or while you are listening to what the person has to say.

A marketing executive once told me that whenever a client pushed back on an idea or argued with him, before responding to the verbal attack, he would make eye contact and say to himself, "I love this guy. He's sharp and bold. I love his conviction."

This Asset-Based Thinking bought him time to think of a great retort, put a smile on his face, lowered his defenses, and got him excited to be in the conversation.

Remember, people have an instinct for whether you are working with them or against them.

Imitate Shamelessly and Often

The fastest way to learn anything is to imitate a role model. Think about how you learned to walk, speak, write the alphabet, and tie your shoes. In the early years, learning by imitation dominates.

For Asset-Based Thinkers, acquiring new insights and skill by imitating the values, beliefs, approaches, and behaviors of individuals they admire is a way of life.

(+) Effective business leaders read biographical articles and books about leaders they admire to learn their secrets to success at the rate of one per week.

(+) Entrepreneurial women accelerate their success threefold by emulating mentors.

(+) Members of the Mankind Project (a world-wide movement dedicated to cultivating greater self-awareness and emotional intelligence among men) have a practice of honoring the legacies of previous generations of men who have paved the way for the current advancements in male consciousness.

Imitating what you admire in others and want to acquire for yourself requires becoming their student, not their judge and jury. As a student of the assets of human nature, you are now ready to spot the best of what anyone has to offer. *Enjoy!*

After-Action Reflection

The U.S. Army debriefs its personnel after major military operations as a way of understanding what works and doesn't and how it might be done differently next time. This after-action review process is an Asset-Based approach that builds on both mistakes and triumphs.

The most reinforcing question you can ask anyone after they accomplished a task is, How did you do that? The question affirms the importance of the accomplishment, but more importantly, it allows a person to reflect on what personal assets (attitudes, knowledge, and skills) were tapped in order to succeed. Whenever you recognize or praise someone in that way, it will last. Encourage conversations that begin with, *How did you do that?* Then keep probing until you gain new insight. Deficit-based thinkers most often ask, *Why did you do that?* . . . setting the stage for a defensive explanation of an action.

Make the affirmative zone work for you!

Take this Asset-Based thought process one step further by asking, How did we do that? to a group. No matter what size the group, posing this question helps them to be alert to what's working to promote satisfaction, inspire collaboration, and produce results. Bring people together in groups to discuss their answers to the question, *How did we do that and that and that and that?* Broadcast the responses. Watch the espirit de corps and collective IQ rise to new levels.

REFLECTION

1. Select one person you interact with on a regular basis (at least twice a week). Pick someone you admire and respect. Reflect on recent experiences you have had together.

2. Zero in on what this person did to stimulate rewarding, productive, enlightening, or humorous interactions.

3. Decide when and how you will communicate your Asset-Based observations to this person. (Communicate through voicemail, telephone, or in person—*not* by e-mail! It lacks emotional intelligence.)

4. Repeat this entire process. Only this time, select a person who frustrates or annoys you. (No kidding—if you do this step, it will change the way you see a whole host of other people who, at the moment, drive you slightly to moderately crazy.)

TIP: If you do this reflection every Friday afternoon, it will help the next week get off to a great start!

notes:

ABT factoid

Ties that bind — Feeling loved intimately and having a trusted confidant contribute to our self-esteem and our sense of mastery—even during high-stress situations. Studies by Irwin Sarason and his colleagues at the University of Washington also reveal that intimate ties with one's spouse make a special contribution to stress resistance.

ABT
WORKOUT
2

ABT principle:
Use Your Positive Filters, Get More Traction

Every type of interaction, from a casual exchange with a clerk at the grocery store to a personal conversation with a good friend to a debate with a colleague, is a perfect time for you to put on your positive filters. Here is how it works:

Step I

Before you interact, take a moment or two to see something about the person that you find valuable, admirable, or interesting. Be specific. Consciously register your positive perceptions by articulating them to yourself. You might say to yourself, "This person has great energy, or an attractive, strong presence, or a calm, confident demeanor."

Note: Research confirms that the tone you set (positive or negative) in the first seven seconds of any interaction determines the predominant tone for the remainder of the interaction. Start well, and you are more likely to end well— even in the face of challenging or disturbing interactions.

Step II

Let your positive perceptions of the other(s) guide what you say and do in the first seven seconds of the interaction. For example, if you have noticed that the person has "great energy," that positive perception might lead you to shake hands with more enthusiasm or to smile more sincerely than you would otherwise. The positive effects of what you say and do will follow suit. It's automatic. Your conscious thoughts about the other person influence how you interact.

Step III

Throughout the interaction, scan and consciously register other things you find positive and interesting. You may become aware that the person also has a great sense of humor, or is a skilled communicator, or displays attractive qualities of conviction and determination. This silent Asset-Based assessment works wonders in any interaction: making decisions, solving problems, setting goals, parenting the kids, discussing politics, or talking baseball. Your ongoing positive commentary about the other person will be the background for what you say and do in the foreground.

Step IV

If an interaction becomes persistently negative and disturbing, finding the positive motives fueling the behavior is a bit more tricky. For example, if someone is making accusations, displaying anger, or complaining, switch to a stronger filter to see through the negativity and identify the positive triggers motivating the behavior. Often anger, accusation, and stonewalling behavior are triggered by frustrated desire for perfection, or to "save the day," or to make things right, or to be more helpful or decisive.

It is far easier to get traction with a person if you speak to the deeper positive motives rather than react to the surface negativity.

Note: If you are not sure which positive motive(s) might be driving the other person's disturbance, just ask yourself, "What might drive me to behave that way?" This assessment can be accomplished in a matter of seconds while you are listening or speaking.

Step V (If needed)

Some people ask, "What do you do when confronted by people driven by greed, arrogance, "my-way-or-the-highway," revenge, or envy? Isn't it important to deal directly with an angry, impulsive, self-serving agenda?" The short answer is *no*. Ignore these negative agendas unless they are fueling abusive, harmful, dangerous behavior. In those rare situations, take time out, remove yourself, call for help—do whatever you need to do to stop interacting until it is safe to do so.

Note: Human beings have a finely tuned Geiger counter. Most (if not all) disturbing behavior is fueled by both positive and negative motives. Engaging the negative motives throws the interaction further off course. Engaging the positive motives gets it back on track.

Linda Gray

Actress, Women's Rights Advocate, Global Change Agent

Linda Gray, known worldwide for her award-winning portrayal of Sue Ellen Ewing on "Dallas," decided to use her talent and celebrity to help the cause of women's rights. Linda was named Ambassador of Goodwill for the United Nations Population Fund and travels the world championing universal access to health care, education, employment opportunities and gender equality for all women. In a recent interview with Kathy, Linda shares her Asset-based secrets for building strong relationships in life and on the job.

Kathy: I've been amazed by the breadth and depth of your life's work and your passion. How do you manage to keep yourself "up" and positive.

Linda: I am like the weed that grows up through the concrete cracks, with a little of Lucille Ball thrown in. We can all choose how we get through the day, the hour, and the moment. I choose to be "in joy" — not la-la land, not a birthday party — but inner joy that comes from a deep appreciation and thankfulness for what life offers.

K: How do you find your inner joy in the midst of the challenging, fast-forward life you (and the rest of us) lead?

L: I certainly have my share of ups and downs and heartbreaks. We all do. I've had to really examine my belief that inner joy is a choice and concluded that it definitely is. I can tap into it and bounce back from negative situations by keeping myself grounded and doing my inner core work.

K: What do mean by your inner core work?

L: I ask myself "what do I want?," "who am I?," "what am I grateful for?" My answers to these questions bring me right back. It never fails me.

K: How did you manage to choose inner joy during all those years on Dallas?

L: Kathy, I can assure you that no course, no university, could prepare you for becoming an overnight success. Your life is turned upside down and there are no mentors to help.

K: It sounds like you had to constantly keep yourself grounded to keep your own identity intact.

L: Yes. I had no choice but to find my inner self every day and move ahead. Also, having a sense of humor about it all made it work for me.

K: You still work in television and the theatre. Do you miss acting full-time?

L: I love acting. It still is a big part of my life, but it's a reality that there are only a few great scripts for older women. But who wants to be a victim?

So now I pick and choose my parts very carefully and put the rest of my energies into being an advocate for women's health and doing things that are even more exciting. Also, hardly a day goes by that I don't meet or hear from a Dallas fan, so that connection is always there.

K: What is it like to meet your Dallas fans today?

L: Dallas fans are really lovely, respectful people. They smile when they recognize me, maybe ask for an autograph, and always tell me a Friday night Dallas story — how it got them through labor, or how special it was to sit with Mom and watch. I love these conversations.

K: What makes interacting with other people so touching and compelling for you?

L: I am fascinated and curious about the connections and stories we all have. I want to be fully present so I can really see the person and make eye contact. Eye contact is my connection.

K: You have become an active leader in the field of women's rights and health, worldwide. Where does your call to service come from?

L: My desires to serve worthwhile causes has always been there. I am a heart-based person. On my first trip to Nicaragua, when I saw the condition of women and children there, I felt the expansion of my compassion right before my eyes. I went to my hotel room and cried every night. I wrote in my journal and asked myself, "How can I help?," "Am I interfering?," "If the 13-year old who was prostituting herself to help feed her household were my child, what would I do?"

K: It comes back to your belief in the power of connections, doesn't it?

L: Yes, very much so. These women tell me their stories and the connection just happens. It is almost like we are connected and joined by one common beating heart. It's very powerful.

K: It feels like those experiences are still with you.

L: Absolutely. The women we serve only want three things: water, healthy childbirth, and education. Every time I see a bottle of water in L.A. I realize how fortunate we are, and how much more work there is to do to bring water and well being to people everywhere.

K: Linda, your determination to create your life—a rewarding, meaningful life, no matter what, is inspiring. Thank you for giving us a glimpse of how you do that.

www.lindagray.com
Check out Linda's website.

To build stronger relationships, connect with the "story" behind what people say and do, as Linda Gray does so well and so often. Someone's story carries meaning because it reveals personal motives, aspirations, and vulnerabilities which brings their assets into focus. Once you see people from the inside out, they become irresistibly interesting. Eli Weisel, Nobel Prize winning theologian, once said, "God invented people because he loves stories."

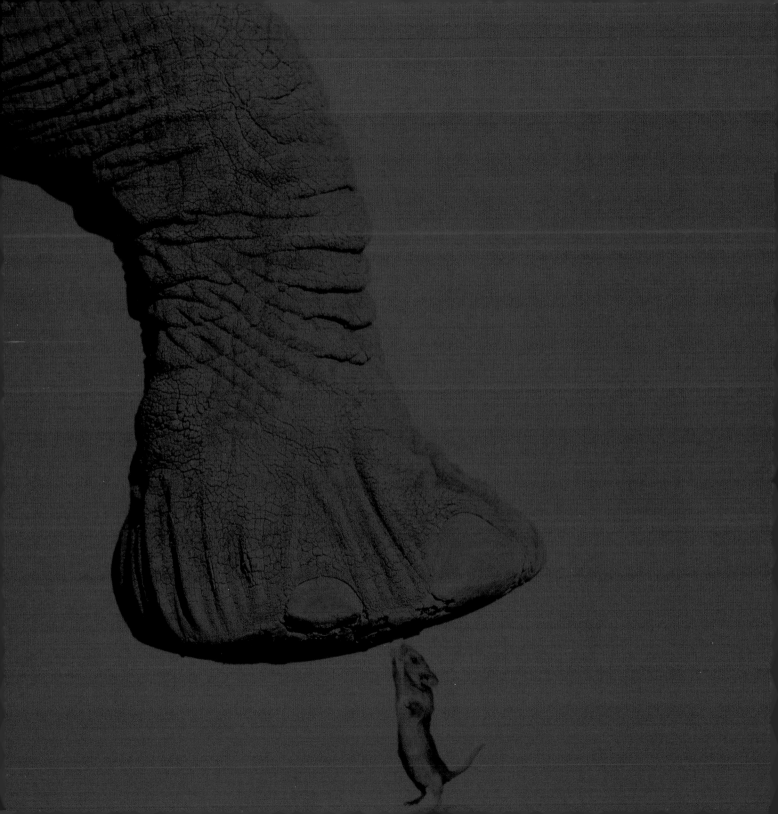

CHANGE THE WAY YOU SEE SITUATIONS

CHANGE THE WAY YOU SEE SITUATIONS

Part III: Preview

Marcia and Ed's stories, which follow, demonstrate how they were able to seek and see opportunities in their situations. The principle of the Wider the Lens the Better the View can be effectively applied to any situation, welcome or unwelcome. The result is a bigger, brighter, and better view that benefits you and those around you. In Marcia's case, she viewed the computer conversion as an opportunity in and of itself. She could have stopped there, but instead, Marcia expanded the field of opportunities by linking the development of her leadership and communication skills to the successful conversion rollout.

On a far more serious note, Ed's story shows how even a major illness can be seen as the chance to deepen one's resolve to live and work passionately. Any reminder of mortality has the power to put us in touch with why we should love life so much. Facing this reality can illuminate what we really value and want to contribute and accomplish.

For Asset-Based Thinkers like Ed, looking through the lens of a life-threatening illness turns daily moments into gifts of time. Time for loving who and what we love. Time for reflecting and taking stock. Time for playing. Time for saying "thank you" and "I'm sorry" and "hurray." Time for wondering what's next and who we really are.

When you encounter trials and tribulations, remember that initial feelings of anxiety are natural, but limiting. The alarm/alert reaction narrows your perspective. It prevents you from seeing countless opportunities to expand your own competencies and strengthen relationships as you deal with daily challenges and happenstance. Part III offers numerous ways to unearth and enhance the benefits associated with whatever happens. Apply the principles and practices of ABT outlined in Part III, and you will eliminate the situational blind spots brought on by anxiety-provoking circumstances.

Marcia's Story

As the chief technology officer of a top-tier pharmaceutical company, I faced a major challenge in the implementation of a comprehensive computer conversion process. I had to overcome the skepticism of more than 2,500 employees, win over their hearts and minds, and make them believers. I knew that the conversion process presented a steep learning curve for everyone involved, but without the employees' commitment and strong buy-in, the implementation would bog down and fail. But, if I could pull it off, this was my big chance to make a significant contribution to expanding the research and sales capabilities of my company.

The big kick-off meeting day was here. I was ready to go and was gearing up for a great PowerPoint presentation filled with facts, figures, strategies, and goals. All of my training in how to make sure the content of my message was clear and the logic of the process airtight was kicking in. Interestingly, about a month before, I had taken an Asset-Based Thinking speaker development course called "Power and Presence." It was very provocative and an interesting departure from all of my past "PowerPoint" thinking training.

I wanted to push the envelope on this opportunity, so I put myself into an ABT mindset: The true power of persuasion lies in the impact the speaker has on the audience, not the presentation. I stayed focused on the thought that my PowerPoint deck, no matter how well written, was just a means to my end. Persuade, motivate, and move the audience to embrace challenge, be part of the solution, and take action.

In every speech, I focused my attention on the audience and read reactions in real time. If I saw or sensed skepticism or confusion, I altered what I said on the spot. I managed to engage hundreds of people at a time in a real exchange because I made the impact of what I said matter more than the content or the perfection of my delivery.

I saw every speaking situation as a chance to expand my expertise and repertoire as an effective, high-impact speaker and made what was happening in the audience the most important focus of my attention and interaction. By widening my lens to see the larger opportunities (honing my leadership and presentation skills and "selling" the computer conversion), my commitment to the project, the company, and my personal growth and development grew exponentially.

Ed's Story

I've always been lucky my whole life. Great parents, great Jesuit schooling, great wife, Jane, and daughter, Lauren, and a beyond-belief successful career.

Throughout my life I've always valued people at all levels and deeply believed that involving, caring, and communicating connects leaders to their organization and yields amazing results.

Having an outlook of always doing better, everything could be improved has been both a strength and a frustration for me and my colleagues: My team mates would ask "Aren't you ever satisfied?" My reply; "Yes, but we need to do better, improve, be competitive to stay on top".

Then, on a business trip, at age 52, friends noticed I didn't look well. Little did I know I would be diagnosed with pancreatic cancer. Completely unexpected. I was challenged like never before.

I now had my biggest challenge ever—overcoming cancer that has a 20% survival rate. Connection to people would be key. Help came to me from many many places, people whom I had forgotten offered help; contacts, prayer, humour, food, whatever could help.

Speed and decisiveness took over. Seven hours of surgery, six months of chemotherapy, five weeks every day of radiation and chemotherapy.

I never asked, "Why did I get cancer?" It served no purpose. The key was to look forward, problem solve and find the necessary strength. My strength came from people; close family, colleagues, and friends from all over the world.

100|

Lance Armstrong has long been one of my heroes. Like him I believe you have to train for life and performance. Fitness, nutrition and enjoyment of life's great moments are essential. This belief also helped me battle cancer.

Outlook and attitude are everything. My wife told me I would be part of the 20% survivors. My oncologist said we'd work together to see my first grand-child and my boss, CEO of the world's biggest food company, said "we'll wait for your return, you'll continue to be responsible".

Today, I'm back at work, cancer free after a nine-month battle. I've never been happier. Every day is wonderful. We only fully appreciate things when they risk being lost.

My life is somewhat changed; it's crystallized, more focused, clearer and simpler. People and their connections gave me the strength to believe even the biggest challenge could be overcome.

All of this life so far continues to be lucky in the most positive sense. A positive attitude, and believing anything is possible through people. Their support, love, cheerleading and amazing capabilities are incredibly powerful.

Above all, having within my spirit that neverending passion—
A PASSION TO WIN!

The Wider the Lens, the Better the View

Keep your senses wide open. Don't miss a detail, pattern, or nuance that will make the difference between just getting by and pulling out all the stops.

In the face of problematic or promising situations, the formula is the same. Look long. Look wide. Look at what's behind and what's in front of you. Look to the left. Look to the right. Examine the situation. Determine the problems and see through them. Extract the opportunities. Be relentless in searching every angle. The more you see, the more you have to work with.

Asset-Based Thinking begins in the privacy of your own mind. Every thought you have about a given circumstance leads to Asset-Based actions and interactions. The conversations you have with yourself about what is possible and worthwhile shapes and frames the exchanges you have with others. Asset-Based Thinking widens and sharpens your personal frame of reference, so you can enlarge the perspective of others. This allows the combined talents and strengths of multiple Asset-Based thinkers to grow exponentially, making it possible to see and harvest an amazing array of benefits. Remember, benefits better the view . . . every view, every time.

Shift From Threat to Challenge

"Tomorrow New York is going to be here. . . and we're going to rebuild, and we're going to be stronger than we were before . . . I want the people of New York to be an example to the rest of the country, and the rest of the world, that terrorism can't stop us." –Rudy Giuliani

Just Breathe!

Whenever a problem arises, your first gut reaction may be alarm. Your body's natural defense mechanism switches on, and all systems are armed and aimed at fighting or fleeing the threat. Every communication breakdown, missed deadline, and costly mistake heightens your focus as you feel a shot of adrenaline restricting your thoughts and speeding your actions. What you may not be aware of is that your breathing changes too. Your breathing becomes shallow (from your chest, not your abdomen) and the intervals between breaths are much shorter (not so short that you are hyperventilating, but shorter).

A simple yet powerful tool you have at your disposal is breath control—the ability to shift your body out of a threat reaction into a challenge response by focusing on your breath. Slow it down. Taking five or six deeper breaths should do the trick. Breathing deeply and slowly facilitates Asset-Based Thinking. You become more creative and less reactive. It puts you in charge of dealing more effectively with the threat at hand. It triggers the excitement of being challenged and dissolves the fear of being threatened. *Try it!*

See the Problem as a Pause

Often when you're witnessing an emergency situation or traumatic event, consciousness becomes heightened and kicks into slow motion. Colors become more vivid, sound disappears, time stops and shifts. This is called state of alarm consciousness. State of alarm consciousness is an extension of the initial alarm reaction to imminent threat or danger. It is a tremendous asset that allows people to respond sharply and swiftly under an extreme pressure to perform.

Those who regularly perform under high-stress conditions—athletes, actors, soldiers, etc.—report similar experiences in anticipation of what may happen next. You can actually replicate this state of awareness whenever a problem pops up and impedes your progress. Simply pause the problem—see it in **slow motion**. This allows you the chance to observe what's really happening. Filter out the distractions, solve the problem fast, and get on with doing what's most important.

Vigilance is a virtue. But don't go overboard. Sometimes the best solution is to ignore the problem or work around it. Don't get overwhelmed by problems or their sometimes intimidating solutions. It's not worth it. See the problem as a pause. Find other ways to move toward the goal.

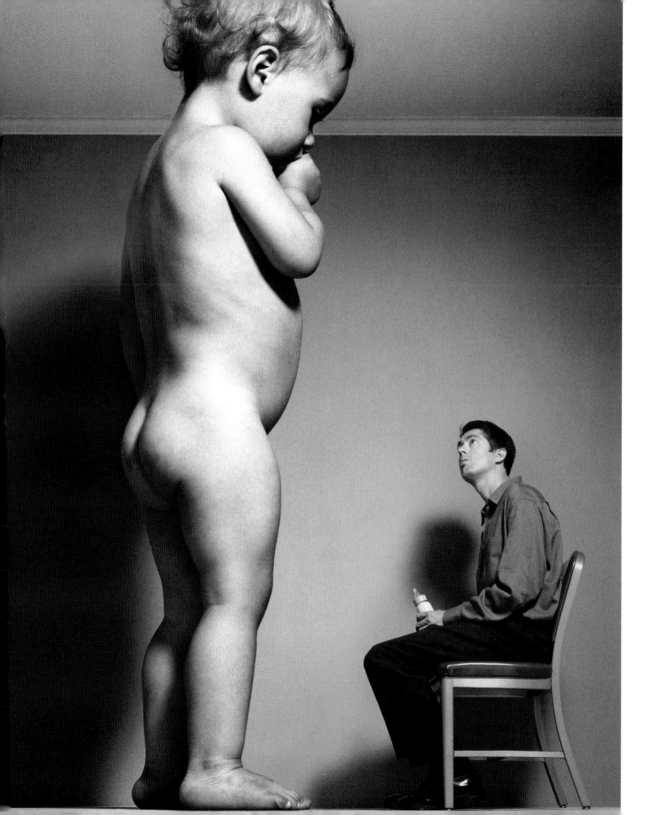

Avoid the
80-20 trap

Apply the 80-20 rule in reverse. Instead of focusing 80 percent of your attention on problems and 20 percent on opportunities, concentrate 80 percent on opportunities and 20 percent correcting what's wrong. This bold mental shift in perspective offers incredible built-in advantages:

(+) To shift your perspective from deficits to assets is to live life differently, unconventionally, even courageously. When you put more of your focus on progress than on perfection, on possibilities than on problems, you challenge the dogmatic and deficit-based thinking in yourself and others.

(+) To most of us, facing a problem usually provokes us to cast blame and assign guilt. But what if you could reach into the depth of that problem and extract a treasure—a wealth of information that could propel the situation forward in a way that benefits everyone involved, exponentially! This moves you into the affirmative zone in which Asset-Based Thinkers thrive.

Sister Wendy Beckett, a contemplative Roman Catholic nun, celebrated art commentator, and media star, once told Bill Moyers, "I don't think being truly human has any place for guilt. Contrition, yes. Contrition means you tell God you won't do it again, you're sorry. Guilt means you go on beating your breast. You're just sitting in a puddle splashing."

Making amends for flawed actions, YES! Making amends for flaws, NO! Feeling guilty in either case, NEVER! Asset-Based Thinking makes you consider your flaws, shortcomings, and limitations as important to who you are and what you have to work with. You see them as the complement to your talents, strengths, and capabilities.

< Hindsight + Insight = Foresight >

We've all heard Nietzche's famous phrase, "That which doesn't kill you makes you stronger" (whether you knew it was Nietzche or not). However, in the middle of a traumatic event, when you lose a job, go through a divorce, make a costly mistake, or suffer a big disappointment, the phrase is a small consolation.

You naturally zero in on the deficits (e.g., what's missing, what's broken, what's not working, what's out of kilter, and out of whack) so you can think your way out of the difficulty and restore equilibrium. The primary aim of deficit-based thinking is to right what is wrong and get you back to even. It's essentially a zero-sum game.

If you want to move beyond zero so that your problem actually yields benefit and puts you in the plus column, then Asset-Based Thinking is what's required.

Many people attest to the fact that in hindsight, suffering the blows of their worst, most challenging disappointments and defeats have handed them some of their most valuable lessons and helped them to **create a positive G.A.P.**

years of smiling

Gratitude: For those people who hung in there or who dove in to help.
Appreciation: For the bounty and blessings life and living have to offer
Perspective: Which priorities are really most important?

These benefits are most clearly seen in hindsight. What if you went looking for them in the midst of dealing with tough situations and major setbacks? Or better yet, what if you could anticipate them using foresight?

When Asset-Based Thinking dominates how you look at experiences (past, present, and future), you can turn turmoil to your advantage sooner. Seeing your sense of purpose, mastery, courage, and determination before, during, and after you encounter difficulty is incredibly rewarding. The encouragement of discovering who is on your side, who can help, and who can be committed to the cause is well worth the search ahead of time.

CREATE THE FUTURE
HERE & NOW

"I am enough of an artist to draw freely upon my imagination.
Imagination is more important than knowledge.
Knowledge is limited. Imagination encircles the world."
– Albert Einstein

Einstein believed that visual understanding must precede all other forms of education. In his younger years, he was thoroughly schooled in mind's-eye visualization: seeing and feeling a physical situation, tangibly manipulating the elements, and then observing (in his imagination) the consequences of his "thought experiments."

Einstein actually pretended to be a photon moving at the speed of light. Mentally, he stepped inside the photon to imagine what he could see and feel from inside. Then he became a second photon and tried to imagine what he would experience from interacting with the first one.

Perception Creates a Longer Reality

Your perception of aging may also impact how long you live. The August 2002 issue of the *Journal of Personality and Social Psychology* reports that older individuals who viewed aging as a positive asset lived seven and a half years longer than those who had a negative view of aging.

ABT factoid

116

Join the Horizon Dwellers

Although most dot.com businesses failed, the founders of eBay visualized a way to appeal to the integrity, competitive spirit, and creativity of their online buyers and sellers and succeed in leveraging a "trust-based" Internet economy. www.**ebay**.com

In the face of one of the most potentially devastating product-tampering cases, the CEO of Johnson & Johnson made the bold move of recalling every bottle of Tylenol from retail shelves, living by the credo of his company. "We believe our *first responsibility* is to the doctors, nurses and patients, to mothers and fathers and all others who use our products and services. In meeting their needs everything we do must be of high quality." Today, the Tylenol brand is stronger than ever. www.**jnj**.com

When other web based search engines were scrambling to build their user and revenue base, Google put its resources into building a demonstrably better search engine. They followed the credo with which they launched their company, "Be in service to our users." A great example of an extraordinary company founded and run on ABT principles. www.**google**.com

Remember: Everything that happens in your day is an exchange between the external world and your internal world. Think of it as raw material replenishing itself everyday. Every situation, every encounter, every person (including you) possesses valuable assets—they are always there in some form and magnitude. Asset-Based Thinking helps you find them.

With Asset-Based Thinking, you discover the possibilities, detect the strengths, mine the resources, and create positive momentum. It's at your disposal. With deficit-based thinking, opportunities loom on the horizon, but you deny yourself the opportunity to ever see them.

Imagine It... And You Can Do It!

Great visions live in the imagination before being manifested in the world. Start each morning with a vivid "mental movie" of what you envision to be the next, best version of your life. This includes aspects of yourself (mental, physical, emotional, spiritual), of your relationships with other people, and the way you further your achievements in the world. Turn yourself on by sharpening your vision. It will give you the feeling of being on purpose, having traction, and creating the life you want every day.

Remember this: Having vision makes life more meaningful and integrated. Be sure to integrate the themes of intimacy, spirituality, and legacy as you turn on the next best vision of your life. Research shows that pursuing these themes makes significant contributions to personal health and well-being.

Intimacy: Set goals that develop your capacity to relate and express a desire for close, reciprocally rewarding relationships, e.g., help friends and let them know you care. Accept others as they are. Listen with as much passion as you speak.

Spirituality: Aim for ways of transcending yourself, e.g., deepen your relationship with God. Notice and appreciate your windfalls and blessings whatever they might be. Celebrate anything wonderful around you. Dwell on what inspires you.

Legacy: Envision contributions you can make to future generations, e.g., be a good role model. Do volunteer work that enhances your community. Mentor, Guide, Help, Care.

Laws of Attraction

A magnetized piece of iron will lift twelve times its own weight. But demagnetized, it won't even lift the weight of a feather.

Your mind works in a similar way. Magnetized with Asset-Based Thinking, you embody the "Laws of Attraction." This means that what you think, say, and do attracts an enormous number of external assets (the commitment, support, and dedicated efforts of other people, the inherent advantages, benefits, and rewards of every situation). At the end of a day of Asset-Based Thinking, you have attracted and stockpiled a rich reservoir of resources ready to be combined and invested for a great return.

Use Asset-Based Thinking to connect with the assets in your reservoir. Link your passion, vision, and skill set with the strengths and capabilities of those you have attracted into your circle of influence. Next, notice how that particular continuation of individual assets connects with the potential in a given situation. *Voila!*

Note: Deficit-based thinking demagnetizes you. It sets in motion the "laws of repulsion." You move through the day trying to live life unscathed. Deficit-based thinking keeps people at bay and rarely attracts anyone to your cause for long. Focusing on problems, barriers, setbacks, and breakdowns is demotivational over time, unless of course your survival is at stake.

ABT
BUSINESS QUIZ

Each day, business situations arise that require us to be flexible in our actions and draw more deeply on our own capabilities, build team spirit, develop underperforming employees, etc. Asset-Based Thinking won't eliminate these challenges, but it will help us deal with them faster and more effectively and, enhance our effectiveness and sense of value. Here are examples of how looking through our Asset-Based Thinking lenses can work.

Which person would you rather work with?

[Deficit-Based Thinker]

This was my best sales day ever. I know home runs are mostly luck. I don't want to get my hopes up too high, and I certainly don't want my regional manager to expect more than I can deliver. I'll keep this success below the radar so that I don't set myself up for an impossible goal next year.

People in this organization are chronic complainers. They whine about almost everything. I wish they'd just get over it, move on and implement the plans that we laid out for them.

The business downturn robbed us of revenue we were counting on and caused some of our best customers to cancel orders. We'll have to retrench and cut our projections for this fiscal year.

[Asset-Based Thinker]

This was my best sales day ever. Last week, I hit two home runs. I'm on a roll. I can't wait to go over what's working with my regional manager. Hopefully, he'll give me additional resources to develop new customers and duplicate the results. If I set the bar realistically higher, I can earn a bigger bonus next year.

People in this organization lack the confidence it takes to get through tough times. I know our plans are strong. How can I win over a few more converts and make their confidence contagious?

The business downturn hurt, but it helped us better identify our most loyal customers. It reminded us of how important it is to stay connected to them and keep our incentive programs flexible and current. It's also energized us to find five new customers to make up the deficit.

REFLECTION

1. Recall the events of your day. List them in sequential order.

2. Recount the story of your day from a negative, deficit-based perspective. Be specific. (For example, *I was late for my first appointment. Not only did being stuck in traffic throw off the rhythm of my whole day, being late reminded me of the fact that I am late too often and I must find a way to correct that bad habit!*) Go ahead, write (or tell someone else) the deficit-based version of today's events—it's cathartic!

3. Next (you guessed it)—recount the story of your day from a positive, Asset-Based perspective. Be sure to describe the same sequence of events. (For example, *I was late for my first appointment. Being stuck in traffic gave me a chance to start the meeting by cell phone in the taxicab. We were lucky to have a clear connection all the way. Starting the day this way reminded me that being flexible counts and that I am not in charge of traffic patterns.*) You will notice a distinct, positive difference in how you are feeling after recalling the ABT version of your day.

4. Try this now.

5. *Voila!* Completing this exercise should convince you that indeed you are able to change the way you see any situation (at least we hope you are intrigued).

notes:

ABT factoid

Matters of the Heart Matter to Health — Research psychologist David McClelland and his colleagues at Boston University conducted a series of studies in which feelings of love and affection for other people were seen to create a stable increase in salivary immunoglobulin, an immune function response. This could very well mean that, over time, loving thoughts and images can increase our resistance to getting sick.

ABT
WORKOUT
3

ABT principle: The Wider the Lens, the Better the View
Here is how to widen your lens in the face of everyday adversity:

Learn to agree with what happens. See reality clearly, accept it, and problem solve from that vantage point. To agree with your reality does not imply that you must be thrilled with annoyance or setbacks. You can have an accepting attitude without endorsing or reveling in them. With these steps, you will widen your lens and better your view.

Step I
Monitor your first thoughts when you encounter adverse situations such as a traffic jam, missed deadline, or personal disappointment. If your thoughts are argumentative, e.g., "I can't believe this! What did I do to deserve this? I'll show them!," give yourself a chance to widen your lens.

Step II
Widen your view by asking yourself, "What is troubling me about this situation?" (Be realistic and specific, e.g., "I want to be on time and now I will not arrive on schedule," or "I was disappointed that he failed to call because I was counting on a dinner date.") Then ask yourself, "What are my opportunities and possibilities now?" e.g., "I can prepare for my meeting while I'm sitting in this traffic and arrive in a good mood," or "I can call someone else for a night out or find a good book and relax."

Step III
Finally, generate action geared toward minimizing the downside of the situation and generate other actions aimed at maximizing the upside of the situation. Ask yourself this open-ended question, "What if I were to … ?" (Be creative with your answers: e.g., "… listen to a great audiotape and rehearse my agenda?" or "… call Bill—I haven't seen him in ages?")

In the face of adversity or opportunity, when you widen your lens (your perspective), the view (what's possible) gets better and better. Narrow perspective limits your options. Panoramic perspective expands your chance of capitalizing on whatever is happening.

The notion of having "blind spots" is a familiar one. In addition to the actual blind spot in our peripheral vision (because of the way our optic nerve functions), most people find they have mental blind spots when it comes to qualities in themselves (both shortcomings and long suits) that others more readily see. When faced with challenging situations (whether welcome or unwelcome), our automatic alarm/alert reactions tend to create "situational blind spots." Situational blind spots conceal the wide array of assets (what we have to work with and build on) in every situation. Apply the principle, the Wider the Lens, the Better the View, and you will eliminate situational blindness once and for all.

Here is how to widen your lens so that you don't miss out on everyday opportunities:

Illuminating the possibilities and opportunities that abound in everyday circumstances increases your options, energizes situations, and inspires you and others. Here is how to see more and more possibilities and fewer and fewer problems.

Step I

At any given moment, in the privacy of your own mind, assess what is working, what is moving forward, what has opened up, and your progress. Make these observations even if there are all-consuming front-burner issues that are dominating your attention. Use your mind like a split screen TV—watch how you are handling the immediate issues *and* note what has facilitated your progress, opportunities that have arisen, and how you have leveraged them.

Step II

Focus on the matters at hand and the context within which you are operating. Ask yourself, "What other opportunities are available? What options have I missed that I could engage and run with?"

Step III

Look ahead. What is in store for you in the hours to come? Get a glimpse of what you are moving into and how your immediate future will serve you.

MOBY & KELLY AT TEANY
Artists, Friends, Entrepreneurs

Moby is enormously successful as a cutting-edge music star and he is also creating "hits" with ventures beyond music. Moby applies some simple yet profound thinking to stay "out in front" of situations and ahead of the curve. He turns things on their head and looks at them from his unique perspective: "what would I like, what would my friends want that they don't know about yet." Moby and his business partner, Kelly, did just that when they opened their restaurant, Teany, in New York City.

Hank: Here we are at Teany, drinking tea and having a great conversation, and it's my understanding that neither of you have restaurant experience! How did you make this happen?

Moby: Well . . . quasi. Neither one of us have had any experience opening a restaurant. I washed dishes in a restaurant at Macy's in Connecticut, and Kelly worked in a bar in Boston where they served deep-fried food.

H: Not exactly the type of restaurant experiences that would drive a person to open a vegan-friendly teahouse in New York.

M: For some reason, I have this irresistible urge to throw myself into things that I know nothing about.

H: So Kelly, you both decided to open Teany, and then Moby went on tour and left it in your hands.

Kelly: I was so nervous, because when Moby left to go on tour, Teany was completely raw space. But, we both had this vision and were determined to make it happen.

H: Was Moby's leaving on tour a blessing in disguise for you?

K: Yes. Definitely.

M: She did everything. Basically I went on tour and came back and we had a finished restaurant. Now I just come here and reflect in the glory of Kelly's work. I eat and play Scrabble with my friends, but I actually don't do any work.

K: Not exactly. If someone walks in and is not greeted right away, Moby is greeting them, getting them menus, and clearing tables.

H: A lot of celebrities open restaurants, "brand it," and then bow out. You have consciously not done that!

M: We wanted to go against that practice and keep my involvement very subtle. And because we are so provincial, our idea was to open a restaurant in our neighborhood that we would enjoy with our friends. That's what guided us.

K: This really is a neighborhood place. It's nice to get out of town visitors, but for the most part, our customers live around here and come in every day.

H: The restaurant opened in the summer, and you didn't feature iced tea on the menu. What happened?

K: It was really a huge oversight. We didn't even think of iced drinks. So I whipped up a few iced tea flavors for our thirsty customers. Then Moby had the idea to combine our teas with juices and spices.

M: Kelly's first reaction was, "Nobody's going to want that," but she humored me, and here we are!

H: Right. First a restaurant, then you launch bottled iced tea . . . probably one of the most competitive categories there is. What were you thinking?

M: Well that's result of a combination of blind self-confidence, a bit of hubris, and complete cluelessness. We figured, hey we opened a restaurant and neither one of us knew anything about opening a restaurant, so why not go into the bottled iced tea world with no experience. We believe very strongly in what we are doing; and that we have a wonderful product people will love. We are still clueless.

H: I am fascinated with the simplicity of the label and the copy you wrote for it.

M: Everyone's initial response was, who is going to have the time to read all that text. My thought was, imagine you get on the subway or a bus and drink your Teany. You have a fifteen to twenty minute ride so this is the perfect time to read. You also have a little cartoon there, so you can play with that too.

H: Interestingly, your huge competitors would never look at it that way.

M: It's true if we were "trained" marketers or living in the suburbs we too would probably say no one will take the time to read the back of an iced tea bottle. But people love it.

H: A year from now, what would make you the happiest about your launch of Teany?

M: Well right now we have three hundred thousand bottles in a warehouse we'd like to sell.

H: First things first.

M: It would be nice to have a business that was succeeding and products people love so we could make more flavors and try new things.

K: We launched with five flavors and have fifteen flavors waiting in the wings. It might sound strange but it's almost like we are in an incubator; we have all these little things growing so we can put them out in the world and see what happens.

M: Yes, we started a restaurant, but we also see it as a "product development laboratory." We didn't want to box ourselves in as far as development potential was concerned.

H: Here's to Teany being a huge success.

M: Let's hope so and that you don't come back a year from now and find Kelly and me living in the alley behind the store.

|131

Think about how Moby and Kelly described the way they see the restaurant and iced tea businesses: "an irresistible urge". . . "open a restaurant in our neighborhood to enjoy with friends". . . "A fifteen-to-twenty-minute ride gives you time to read the label". . . "We have started a product-development laboratory." These comments reveal personal motives and perspectives unique to the individuals involved. Moby and Kelly, by putting themselves in the shoes of the owner and the customer simultaneously, are creating a business that satisfies both sets of needs. What are your unique perspectives and motives that will allow you to create the life and work you desire most?

teany ●

www.**teany**.com
Check out teany's website.

So, What's Next?

Rainbows are circles (really). We only see the upper halves because the horizon hides the rest.

Go beyond the horizon. See the whole rainbow.

To acquire knowledge, one must study;
but to acquire wisdom, one must observe.
-Marilyn vos Savant

ACKNOWLEDGEMENTS

Thinkers Who Inspire . . .

David Cooperrider—founder, professor of psychology at Case Western Reserve, and practitioner of the concept of Appreciative Inquiry, has developed a methodology that assists organizations in shaping their future from the positive core of what already exists and what is already working.

Martin Seligman—professor of psychology at University of Pennsylvania and author of *Learned Optimism, and Authentic Happiness*, scholar and thought leader in understanding optimism.

Mel Levine, M.D.—educator and author of *A Mind at a Time*, an Asset-Based thinker who has contributed significantly to our understanding of individual differences in children's learning styles, skills, and talents.

Marvin Weisbord and Sandra Janoff—creators of the *Future Search* process, and authors of *Future Search*, a methodology to help organizations solve critical problems through this creative and innovative process.

Juanita Brown—founder of the World Café, has spread this ABT process worldwide to help individuals engage in meaningful and important dialogue around questions that matter.

Harrison Owen—founder and creator of *Open Space*, offers this ABT methodology to organizations who want to present at meetings and conferences. It invites everyone present to teach and learn from each other.

William Ury—author of *Getting to Yes*, *Getting Past No*, and *Getting to Peace*. Each of these books demonstrates ways of finding the common ground among people with differences and tapping into the collective strengths and talents of those present.

Mihaly Cziksentmihalyi—professor at University of Chicago, the author of several books including *Flow: The Psychology of Optimal Experience*. He identifies the state of being engaged so fully in what we are doing, with just the right amount of stretch that we are deeply satisfied and literally lose track of time.

meet the people involved with this book . . .

Blake Olsen

Jessica Crimmins

John Gellos

Peggy Guest

James Ioveno

Linda Gray

Ed Marra

Kelly Tisdale

Ray Mendez

Beth Chesterton

Robbie Roxas

John Davis

Will Morrison

Griffin Stenger

Moby

Gosia Anna Kollek

Allen Tamaren

Rebecca Gellos

Colleen Moore

Sonia Manzano

Judy Dubin

Russell Cole

Robert Singh

Getty Images

Chase Rogers

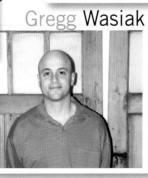

Gregg Wasiak

Denise Marcil

Our Story {

An unlikely collaboration. A successful business consultancy in the heartland and an up-start New York creative company. For over twenty years The Cramer Institute has been studying outstanding people from all walks of life, unlocking their secrets to building extraordinary relationships and making a difference in work and in the world. From this work we developed simple, proven methods of passing these lessons along to others . . . Asset-Based Thinking.

How I see Hank:

Hank is in love with life, people, and making things happen. He is a rare combination: grounded by a well-earned work ethic and values of fairness, commitment and loyalty. Hank is an accomplished executive who believes that he as an individual can make a positive difference in people's lives. When I met Hank he was looking for a big idea that could transform lives for the better. He decided to apply his creativity and marketing savvy to Asset-Based Thinking. His decision was this project's biggest gift. Everyday I am inspired by his energy, enthusiasm, dedication, and the assets he brings to me. His top five as I see them:

Hank's Assets:

Humor - Willing to laugh at himself and life's ironies.
Risk - He rolls the dice. Never lives in the safe lane.
Boldness - I know what he thinks and feels, vibrantly and immediately.
Compassion - His brilliant mind is outdone only by a heart, tender and compassionate.
Possibility-Seeking - Every moment offers a new opening and new opportunity.

Kathy

dr_assets@assetbasedthinking.com

ABT is a mental lighthouse that illuminates the best in a person, relationship, and situation. When this powerful tool was ready to be brought <u>to life</u> and into <u>people's lives</u>, enter The Concept Farm - a team of creative entrepreneurs who founded and built a successful communications company on these ABT principles . . . without knowing it. There was an instant connection around a common passion . . . making the world a better place through Asset-Based Thinking.

}

How I See Kathy:

When I met Kathy I was Vice Chairman of McCann-Erickson and had just finished my training as a Reiki Master. I knew I was on a new and better path but wasn't sure where to take it. Then along came Kathy with her infectious enthusiasm and simple, yet profound advice. She is an incredibly talented and intuitive "coach." Kathy opened my mind, heart and soul to something wonderful . . . Asset-Based Thinking. My life has been forever changed and I thank Kathy for that and the assets she brings to me everyday. Here's her top five as I see them:

Kathy's Assets:

Realness - I trust her totally.
Empathy - We always connect, respect and feel.
Insight - I always learn something new and better.
Calm - She focuses me so I stay on track.
Fun - She always makes me smile and we laugh a lot.

Hank

assetwise@assetbasedthinking.com

● THE CRAMER
INSTITUTE
THE BEST IS NEXT

Come join the positive conspiracy of Asset-Based Thinkers and enjoy the thrill of infusing your every thought, action and interaction with the power of Asset-Based Thinking. ABT works every time and everywhere—at the office, on the train, in a meeting, out for lunch, in the shower. For over twenty years, **The Cramer Institute** has been equipping people from all walks of life with the Asset-Based Thinking tools that have transformed their lives.

Kathryn Cramer received her Ph.D. in Psychology from St. Louis University. In 1980, she founded The Stress Center within the St. Louis University Medical Center and founded The Cramer Institute in 1990. Dr. Cramer is a sought after, leading edge thinker who has successfully led over 300 organizations in adopting Asset-Based Thinking. She published three previous books: *Staying On Top When Your World Turns Upside Down, Roads Home,* and *When Faster, Harder Smarter Is Not Enough.*

The Concept Farm

The farmers at **The Concept Farm** tapped into their creative assets and expertise in broadcast production and digital media to bring a new dimension to the Cramer Institute's AbT tools. These popular seminars, workshops, and coaching practices have been enhanced and expanded making it possible for just about everyone to "connect". Log on to **www.assetbasedthinking.com** and become a positive co-conspirator.

Hank Wasiak is an advertising industry icon who has worked with the corporate elite of global businesses. He was Vice Chairman of McCann-Erickson and then co-founded The Concept Farm, an award winning communications company. Famous for its ground breaking creative work, The Concept Farm has won over 50 International Creative awards including Clios, Cannes Lions and an Emmy.

The Concept Farm

ABT Q CARDS

Use these cards to create
your own ABT Ripple effect.
Start with yourself. Put 'em on the
fridge, under the pillow, on your desk,
in your follow-up file. Whatever.

Then, inspire colleagues, encourage
friends, share them with your family.
Help others make that one small
shift to the asset side of life that will
change the way they see everything.

How do you get a great idea to take off?

SPACESHIP Mk.III.
TO START BOOSTER MOTORS PUT 6" IN SLOT
AND PULL CONTROL ROD SLOWLY BACK

THE SPACESHIP

Did you know that your assets are showing?

Let your assets
and those of others
fuel your passions.

www.assetbasedthinking.com

Wear them proudly.
Let others see who you really are.

www.assetbasedthinking.com

Your assets
take others to the top.

CHANGE
THE WAY YOU
SEE
EVERYTHING

www.assetbasedthinking.com

YOUR ASSETS ARE IN PERFECT BALANCE.

CHANGE
THE WAY YOU
SEE
EVERYTHING

www.assetbasedthinking.com

Assets always better the view.

CHANGE
THE WAY YOU
SEE
EVERYTHING

www.assetbasedthinking.com

Embrace the wealth of assets around you.

CHANGE
THE WAY YOU
SEE
EVERYTHING

www.assetbasedthinking.com

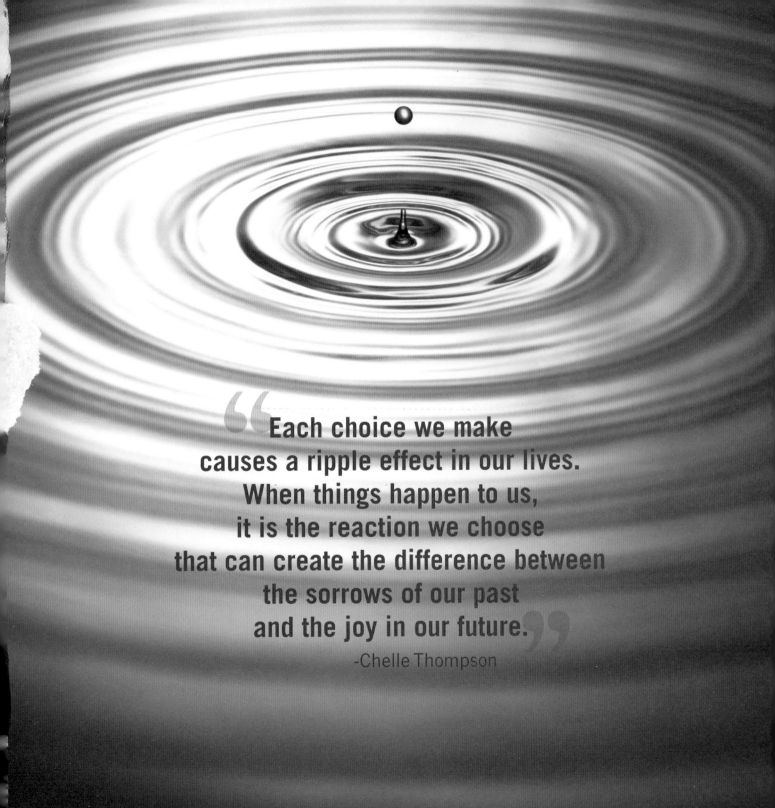

"Each choice we make
causes a ripple effect in our lives.
When things happen to us,
it is the reaction we choose
that can create the difference between
the sorrows of our past
and the joy in our future."

-Chelle Thompson

WHEN YOU CHANGE THE WAY YOU SEE THINGS, THE THINGS YOU SEE CHANGE.

The image on the following page may look like a photograph of a mountain landscape in the clouds. And in the imagination of an Asset-Based Thinker, it is a mountain landscape. In reality, it is not a photograph of anything. It is a piece of photogenic art created with wax paper, water and light.

Look again. What do you see?